DEEP-SEA EXPLORATION

SCIENCE · TECHNOLOGY · ENGINEERING

BY WIL MARA

CHILDREN'S PRESS®

An Imprint of Scholastic Inc.
New York   Toronto   London   Auckland   Sydney
Mexico City   New Delhi   Hong Kong
Danbury, Connecticut

CONTENT CONSULTANT
Amy Baco-Taylor, PhD, Associate Professor, Department of Earth, Ocean, and Atmospheric Science, Florida State University, Tallahassee, Florida

PHOTOGRAPHS ©: age fotostock: 58 right (John Hyde/Alaska Stock Images), 32, 35 (Joseph C. Dovala); Alamy Images: 3, 46, 47 (AF archive), 25 (Bruce Miller), 22 (David Fleetham), 14 (DIZ Muenchen GmbH, Sueddeutsche Zeitung Photo), 5 right, 55 (epa european pressphoto agency b.v.), 30 (Guenter Fischer/imageBROKER), 53 (Islandstock), 43 (Jeff Rotman), 29 left (John Cairns), 42 (louise murray), 59 (Neil lee Sharp), 13 (Pictorial Press Ltd), 6 (redbrickstock.com), 5 left, 36 (RGB Ventures/SuperStock), 8 (Robert Harding World Imagery), 31 (US Coast Guard Photo); AP Images: 20 (NOAA), 21, 49 (Wilfredo Lee), 27; Corbis Images: 17 (Bettmann), 54 (Federico Scoppa), 37 top (Roger Ressmeyer); Eric Heupel 2012: 24 top; Getty Images: 50 (Jason LaVeris/FilmMagic), 51 (Keipher McKennie/WireImage), 11 right (Otis Imboden/National Geographic), 38 (Photo Researchers), 44 (Saul Loeb), 4 right, 29 right (Stan Honda/AFP), 52 (Vegar Abelsnes Photography); Hawaii Undersea Research Laboratory (HURL)/Max Cremer: 40; John Peter Oleson: 9; Magictorch LTD: cover background; Media Bakery: 37 bottom (DreamPictures/VStock), 34 (Karen Doody); National Geographic Creative: 48 (Emory Kristof), 12 (Norbert Wu/Minden Pictures), 26 (Thomas J. Abercrombie); Newscom/Mark Thiessen: 56; Courtesy Nuytco Research Ltd: cover suit; OceanGate, Inc.: 24 bottom; PLOS One/Sparks et al: cover fish; Science Source: 39 (Alexis Rosenfeld), 16 (NOAA); The Image Works: 18 (J. Chias/V&W), 58 left (Martin Benjamin), 4 left, 15 top (Mary Evans Picture Library), 28 (North Wind Picture Archives), 15 bottom (SZ Photo/Scherl), 11 left (TopFoto), 10 (ullstein bild); Woods Hole Oceanographic Institution: 23 (Tim Shank), 57 (Tom Kleindinst).

LIBRARY OF CONGRESS CATALOGING-IN-PUBLICATION DATA
Mara, Wil, author.
  Deep-sea exploration : science, technology, and engineering / by Wil Mara.
      pages cm. — (Calling all innovators: a career for you)
  Summary: "Learn about the history of deep-sea exploration and find out what it takes to make it in this exciting career field" — Provided by publisher.
  Audience: Age 9–12.
  Audience: Grades 4–6.
  Includes bibliographical references and index.
  ISBN 978-0-531-20536-5 (library binding : alk. paper) — ISBN 978-0-531-21173-1 (pbk. : alk. paper)
1. Underwater exploration — History — Juvenile literature. 2. Ocean — Discovery and exploration — Juvenile literature. 3. Oceanography — Vocational guidance — Juvenile literature. 4. Marine sciences — Vocational guidance — Juvenile literature. I. Title.
  GC65.M337 2015
  551.46'023 — dc23   2014030288

1 2 3 4 5 6 7 8 9 10 R 24 23 22 21 20 19 18 17 16 15

CALLING ALL INNOVATORS

A CAREER FOR YOU

Science, technology, engineering, arts, and math are the fields that drive innovation. Whether they are finding ways to make our lives easier or developing the latest entertainment, the people who work in these fields are changing the world for the better. Do you have what it takes to join the ranks of today's greatest innovators? Read on to discover whether deep-sea exploration is a career for you.

TABLE *of* CONTENTS

The ocean depths are filled with creatures unlike any others on Earth.

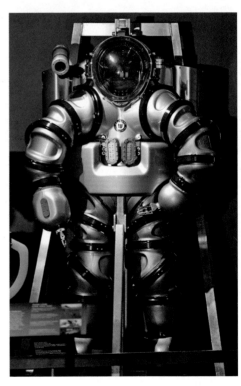

The latest diving suits enable explorers to reach incredible depths.

Deep-sea explorers often record footage of their dives.

James Cameron's DEEPSEA CHALLENGER *set a new standard for deep-sea exploration.*

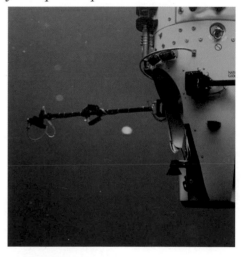

Deep-sea exploration has allowed us
to study a huge variety of marine life.

1

THE WORLD BENEATH THE WAVES

Humans are curious by nature. If something is hidden, we uncover it. Once we've uncovered it, we study it. And after we've studied it, we draw conclusions from it. This is how we have learned so much about our home planet. We've traveled over just about every inch of Earth's land. We've also spent quite a bit of time, energy, and money flying through its skies. But, amazingly, we have barely made a dent in exploring the watery world that covers the majority of the planet. With deep-sea exploration technology now developing at an astounding rate, this is quickly changing.

OCEAN EXPLORERS

1831	**1872**	**1930**	**1960**
Charles Darwin sets sail on the HMS Beagle and collects samples of numerous marine animals.	The HMS Challenger, with chief scientist Charles Wyville Thomson aboard, sets sail on the first significant marine expedition to include deep-sea studies.	William Beebe and Otis Barton become the first humans to reach true deep-sea depths.	Jacques Piccard and Don Walsh are the first humans to reach the floor of the Mariana Trench.

IN THE BEGINNING

Many historians believe that it was the Vikings who got things started with deep-sea exploration. Vikings were Scandinavian seafarers who overran countless European coastal villages from the 700s to the 1000s. When they weren't busy conquering people, they were riding the seas in long, wooden ships. As a result, they were very skilled sailors. With the amount of time they spent on the water, they eventually became curious about the mysterious world beneath the waves. This inspired them to begin the earliest known attempts at deep-sea exploration.

Some Viking ships have been preserved for centuries in museums.

Sounding weights were used by the ancient Greeks and Romans as well as the Vikings.

EARLY EXPERIMENTS

At some point, the Vikings decided that it would be interesting to know just how deep the water was. They also wanted to get some idea of what sorts of objects were beneath the surface. To accomplish both, they used a crude device known as a sounding weight. It was a small, bell-shaped piece of iron with a hollowed-out core attached to a rope. Using the rope, the Vikings lowered the weight into the water until it hit bottom. The Vikings then hauled it back to the surface. On the way up, the weight's hollow core grabbed on to whatever material it struck. This allowed the Vikings to collect samples of aquatic plants, rocks, and other objects. They could also measure how deep the water was simply by measuring how much rope was used. The standard unit of measurement for this practice was known as a **fathom**. It was based on the length of a man's outstretched arms, established then as exactly 6 feet (1.83 meters). The word itself is drawn from the Old Norse word *fathmr*.

PAST MARVELS

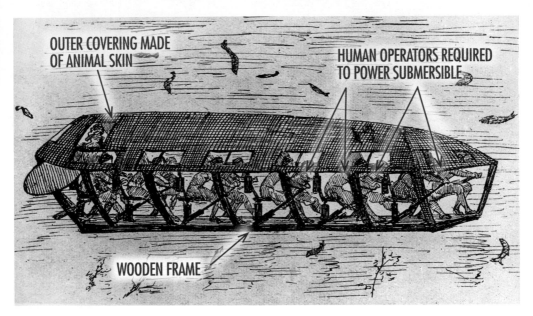

Cornelis Drebbel's submarine design was very simple compared to today's submersibles.

GOING DEEP

Before people could begin exploring the ocean depths, they needed equipment that would allow them to survive far beneath the surface. While diving suits and breathing equipment allow people to survive underwater, they can only go so deep. On the other hand, a **submersible** offers the opportunity for much deeper exploration.

THE DREBBEL SUBMARINE

Cornelis Jacobszoon Drebbel was born in the late 1500s in Alkmaar, Holland. He had tremendous natural abilities in many areas of math and science. As a young man, he built telescopes, eyeglasses, and microscopes. He also contributed to the field of chemistry. But perhaps his best-known creation was the first workable submarine. In 1620, he built a sub with a wooden structure covered by animal skin. It could dive about 15 feet (4.6 m) deep and remain submerged for a few hours. Drebbel continued improving on this design in the following years. His most advanced model could carry more than a dozen people and be steered with oars. The oars stuck out through holes that were sealed with leather.

Piccard's final design was more than 48 feet (14.6 m) long and 20 feet (6.1 m) high. It weighed more than 125 tons. It was put to sea off the coast of Florida in July 1969 and did not resurface until a month later, just south of Nova Scotia, Canada. During that time, Piccard and his crew made detailed and groundbreaking studies of the Atlantic Ocean. ☀

The mesoscaphe changed the way people explored the depths of the ocean.

LONGER JOURNEYS

In the 1960s, Swiss oceanographer and engineer Jacques Piccard began building a new kind of deep-sea submersible. He called it a mesoscaphe. It could remain underwater for long periods of time. It also had enough room for several passengers. These features made it better for extended underwater studies than previous submersibles.

Jacques Piccard poses aboard the submersible Ben Franklin.

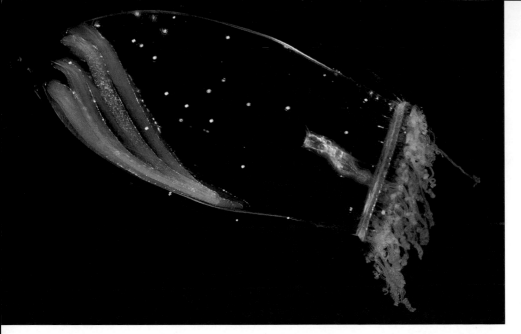

Jellyfish and other amazing animals swim deep below the surface of the Arctic Ocean.

THERE'S LIFE DOWN THERE?

In light of all we know about the oceans today, it's hard to believe there was a time when people thought there was no life down there. But it's true. Throughout much of human history, most people assumed the great seas were nothing but sand and rock covered in water. This began to change in the 1800s.

The first person to start changing the way people thought about ocean life was a man named Sir John Ross. Ross was a British naval officer and sea explorer. In 1818, he began the first of three expeditions into Arctic waters. There, he mapped out formerly uncharted geography and took measurements of water, ice, tides, and currents. He also used sounding weights to collect **specimens** of weird and wonderful undersea creatures that no one had seen before, from depths up to 1 mile (1.6 km) beneath the surface. This was the very beginning of true deep-sea exploration. However, it offered the suggestion that there was a huge variety of life waiting to be discovered beneath the waves.

DARWIN RIDES A *BEAGLE*

Word of Ross's discoveries began to spread through the European scientific community. Soon, a campaign to take the search further gained momentum. In 1831, Captain Robert FitzRoy set out on a voyage aboard the HMS *Beagle* to learn more about marine life. With him was a young scientist named Charles Darwin. The *Beagle's* voyage lasted just under five years. During this time, Darwin kept a diary, made detailed illustrations, and collected numerous specimens. He examined many marine animals. He also set aside hundreds of other specimens to be studied by more-qualified experts upon his return. To capture sea life, he dropped a net into the water and let it drag behind the boat. Darwin also used the ship's extensive library for reference. He became so knowledgeable about certain topics that he ended up making important updates to many of the books.

Charles Darwin gathered important oceanographic data while traveling aboard the HMS Beagle.

SMALL ENTRANCE FOR OPERATOR

William Beebe sits inside the first bathysphere in 1930.

THE GIANT, HOLLOW STEEL BALL

By the dawn of the 20th century, scientists had begun to examine the possibility of sending not just sounding weights but actual people into the ocean's watery depths. The person who turned this idea into reality was an American naturalist named William Beebe. Beebe established a marine research station in Bermuda in 1928. After becoming frustrated with the limitations of ocean exploration technology, he began working with engineer Otis Barton to design a vehicle that could keep a person alive deep below the surface. Barton came up with the **bathysphere**. Put very simply, the bathysphere was a giant, hollow steel ball with windows. Barton decided on the spherical shape because it could resist the tremendous **pressure** that exists at great depths.

SIMPLE TECHNOLOGY

The first bathysphere was equipped with a cable for raising and lowering it into the water, and even a telephone so the diver could communicate with people back on the surface. The bathysphere was first used successfully in 1930. That year, Beebe and Barton went about 800 feet (244 m) below the surface. It was a depth that no human had ever achieved before. Barton continued to improve the vessel, and the pair was able to go even deeper on later dives. Their deepest journey came in August 1934, when they reached a depth of 3,028 feet (923 m). By the end of that year, Beebe considered his studies complete. He did not use the bathysphere again. He and Barton had been able to make groundbreaking firsthand observations of marine life. A new age of deep-sea exploration had begun.

IN THE YEARS SINCE

Beebe and Barton's "Giant Steel Ball" became one of the most important developments in sea-exploration history. It set the stage for all the submersibles to come. Today's deep-sea vehicles have countless technological advantages that these two innovators couldn't have dreamed of, including high-definition cameras, powerful lighting, and even robotic arms. However, the basic physical principles of Barton and Beebe's very first design remain just as useful today as they were back then. Like the bathysphere, modern deep-sea vehicles have reinforced steel walls for protection against the

An illustration showing one of Barton's submersibles exploring the deep sea

pressure of the deep seas, and windows through which divers can get a clear view of their surroundings. ✴

Otis Barton (left) and William Beebe (right) pose next to their bathysphere before a dive in the Atlantic Ocean.

LIGHT ALLOWS PEOPLE INSIDE TO SEE IN DARK DEPTHS OF THE OCEAN

TETHER CONNECTS TO BATHYSPHERE TO LOWER IT INTO WATER

CHALLENGING THE *CHALLENGER*

England led the way again in deep-sea exploration with the launch of the HMS *Challenger* in 1872. The mission was led by Charles Wyville Thomson, a naturalist and marine zoologist. Thomson's goal was to travel nearly 70,000 **nautical** miles around Earth. It was by far the most ambitious expedition of its time.

Thomson wanted to study the deepest parts of the ocean. He was looking to collect data not only on plants and animals, but also on the properties of ocean water itself. He wanted to map parts of the ocean floor as well. At the time, the best method for measuring depth remained similar to that of the Vikings—a weight tied to the end of a rope. As a result, the *Challenger* was equipped with about 180 miles (290 kilometers) of rope. In March 1875, Thomson and his crew made a breakthrough when they became the first humans to discover the Mariana Trench. The trench is a depression found on the floor of the Pacific Ocean off the eastern coasts of China and the Philippines. It is home to the deepest known point on Earth. Floating above the trench's southern tip, the crew measured an astonishing depth of 4,475 fathoms (8,184 meters). The *Challenger*'s mission finished up in 1876, and the information it gathered would go on to form the basis of modern **oceanography**. The deep point it measured is now called the Challenger Deep in honor of the mission.

The HMS Challenger*'s research equipment was state-of-the-art for its time.*

Jacques Piccard sits inside Trieste *during a 1956 dive.*

THE DEEPEST SPOT IN THE WORLD

Building on the bathysphere concept, another two-man team made exploration history in 1960 when they used a similar vehicle to become the first humans to reach the deepest part of the ocean. The vehicle—named *Trieste*—was manned by Jacques Piccard and Don Walsh. They were on a journey to an area known as the Challenger Deep, which sits roughly 7 miles (11 km) beneath the ocean's surface. This is the deepest known point on the ocean floor and is located in the Mariana Trench. It took Piccard and Walsh nearly five hours to reach the bottom. During the descent, one of the outer windowpanes cracked. They were only able to spend about 20 minutes on the seafloor. Nevertheless, they reported seeing small fish swimming about. This surprised some experts who weren't sure whether fish could survive in such intense pressure.

CONNECTED TO SHIP
ABOVE USING TETHER

BREATHING
EQUIPMENT

Technologies such as this metal stage allow divers to easily move up and down through the water.

CHAPTER TWO

WHAT'S AHEAD

The technology for exploring the deep seas has been progressing rapidly in the last few years. Less than a century ago, the idea of reliably gathering data, images, artifacts, and living specimens from the seafloors was little more than a dream. Since those dreamy days, however, we've discovered thousands of new species, located the wreck of the *Titanic* and numerous other sunken ships, and sent people to the deepest parts of the ocean. With these achievements already behind us, just imagine what others await in the future.

DEEP-SEA EXPLORATION SETBACKS

1973	2010	2014
Two crew members of the submersible Johnson Sea Link *die from carbon dioxide poisoning after their vessel becomes trapped in the wreckage of the* USS Fred T. Berry.	Nearly five million barrels of oil flow into the Gulf of Mexico following the explosion and sinking of the Deepwater Horizon oil rig.	The Nereus unmanned craft implodes while exploring the Kermadec Trench.

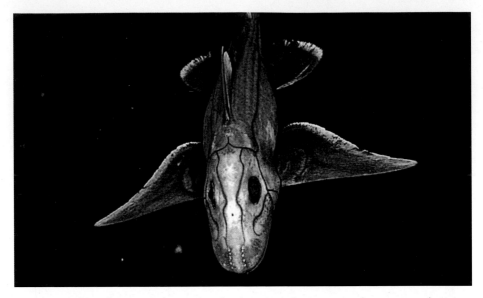

Scientists studying the ocean's deepest trenches have turned up surprising discoveries, such as the chimaera. Surrounded by darkness, this fish "sees" by detecting electrical signals in the water around it.

ANOTHER TRENCH TRIP

The Mariana Trench isn't the only place in the ocean that's really, really deep. In 2013, marine scientists got a chance to explore another undersea region where no human had gone before—the New Hebrides Trench. This trench lies in the Pacific Ocean, along the edge of the Coral Sea, about 1,000 miles (1,609 km) north of New Zealand. The project was a joint effort between the United Kingdom's Oceanlab at the University of Aberdeen and New Zealand's National Institute of Water and Atmospheric Research.

Scientists sent an unmanned vessel about 23,000 feet (7,010 m) under the surface. It was loaded up with lights, high-definition cameras, and bait to lure any creatures that might pass by. Above the surface, the scientists watched the vessel's progress on video screens. They saw an array of scary-looking fish, wiggling eels, and brightly colored crustaceans as the vessel explored.

RISING GRANDSON

One of the most accomplished marine explorers in history was Frenchman Jacques Cousteau, who died in 1997. Cousteau's work was carried on by his grandson, Fabien Cousteau, who is an explorer and aquatic filmmaker. One of Fabien's most notable recent achievements was Mission 31, carried out in June and July 2014. It was a 31-day stay in a human-made underwater laboratory known as Aquarius. Roughly the size and shape of a bus, Aquarius is a fully functional scientific station. It is equipped with computers, communications devices, cameras, and other useful equipment.

Jacques Cousteau had completed a similar mission 50 years earlier when he stayed in the Conshelf II outpost in the Red Sea for 30 days. Fabien made a point of staying underwater just one day longer in order to break the record. He stated that his main goal for the mission was "to reach as many people around the world for 31 days as possible to empower and impassion future generations to care about the oceans, to cherish them, to be curious about them."

Fabien Cousteau waves from inside the Aquarius Reef Base during Mission 31.

MEDICAL ADVANCEMENTS

Exploring the deep seas can be extremely expensive. However, these costs are often rewarded with important discoveries. Many of these findings have even benefited people in major ways. For example, we now know about a sponge in the Caribbean Sea that produces substances needed to make medicine for AIDS treatment. Gorgonian corals, or sea fans, are also commonly tested for medicinal compounds. One species from the Caribbean has been found to produce numerous chemicals that can be used to make pain relief drugs. Along those lines, certain sea snails have venom that works as an effective pain treatment for humans. Other sea creatures even produce compounds that may be useful in the fights against cancer and Alzheimer's disease. It seems clear that we have many reasons to continue to explore the watery underworld of our planet, even if it is costly.

Humans have found uses for many undersea life-forms, including Gorgonian coral.

GORGONIAN CORAL

Nereus *is lowered into the water before a dive.*

A TOUGH BREAK

In spite of all the amazing discoveries people have made in deep-sea exploration, there have also been setbacks in recent times. The deep-sea exploration community suffered a devastating blow in May 2014 when the craft *Nereus* was lost. *Nereus* was an unmanned, untethered underwater vehicle that was operated by remote control. It possessed searchlights, powerful **sonar** scanners, as well as an extendable arm for collecting samples. It made headlines in May 2009 when it reached the deepest part of the Mariana Trench—35,768 feet (10,902 m)—and remained in the area for more than 10 hours. The craft sent back video of previously unseen marine life and seascapes.

Nereus was used for many scientific projects, including one with a goal of locating sea creatures that could help with the treatment of Alzheimer's disease. Scientists hoped it would also provide important data about the Pacific Ocean's Ring of Fire, an area where volcanoes and earthquakes are common. Unfortunately, the tremendous deep-sea pressure caused *Nereus* to **implode** on May 10, 2014, while exploring the Kermadec Trench. Its creators, however, vowed to build an improved version and get right back to work.

Doc Ricketts *and other ROVs can gather data in places that human divers can't reach.*

WHAT'S UP, DOC?

People have been sending unmanned vehicles down into the ocean depths for years, and today's unmanned submersibles boast greater technological capabilities than ever before. One of the most advanced is the ROV *Doc Ricketts*, currently being used by Monterey Bay Aquarium Research Institute. ROV stands for "remotely operated vehicle." Because ROVs do not carry people, they can remain underwater for long periods and travel to places that would normally be considered too dangerous for humans. In most cases, an ROV is attached to a ship on the surface with a **buoyant**

cable called a tether. These cables allow scientists on the ship to communicate with the ROV. They also provide the vehicle with

electricity. *Doc Ricketts* also has tool kits that can be modified to suit different projects, movable high-definition cameras, a range of data-collecting sensors, and other useful equipment. It was named for Dr. Ed Ricketts, a famed marine biologist.

THE *CYCLOPS 3000*

In May 2013, OceanGate, a company that focuses on advancements in sea exploration, announced plans to create a revolutionary new submersible called *Cyclops 3000*. It is being built with the help of the University of Washington's Applied Physics Lab. *Cyclops 3000* will be large enough to carry a crew of five, which sets it ahead of most other deep-sea submersibles. It will also have a depth range of about 9,840 feet (3,000 m). The craft will be constructed from lightweight materials. This means it will use less energy and be more **maneuverable** than other submersibles. According to OceanGate, the purpose of the *Cyclops 3000* is to "travel to the oceans' depths for myriad tasks and operations, including environmental assessments, inspection, equipment testing, mapping, data collection, and overall subsea operations." OceanGate hopes to have the first working model ready for action in 2016.

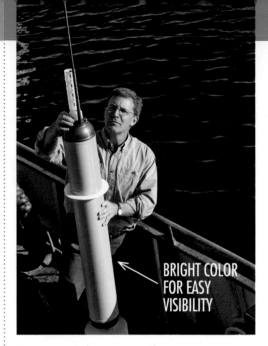

BRIGHT COLOR FOR EASY VISIBILITY

An oceanographer examines the measurement devices on an Argo float.

FLOATS

One of the more remarkable tech devices from the world of oceanographic exploration is the profiling float. This is a buoy that is programmed to collect data and then transmit it to a base station. There are thousands of these machines drifting around in the oceans today. The average profiling float picks up information about water temperature, motion, pressure, density, and more using its onboard sensors. Once enough information is gathered, scientists will begin to see patterns and gain a better understanding of certain oceanographic areas. One of the most widespread systems is known as Argo. It began in the early 2000s and now has more than 3,500 profiling floats around the world. ✳

Jacques Cousteau introduced countless people to deep-sea exploration through his many projects.

IN THE COMFORT OF YOUR OWN HOME

Do you want to explore the deep seas of the world but can't wait until you're old enough to run your own expedition? Well, thanks to today's technology, you might not have to wait any longer than the time it takes to turn on your computer, tablet, or smartphone. In recent years, the National Oceanic and Atmospheric Administration (NOAA) has begun live-streaming their journeys to the public. If you have an Internet connection, you can sit back and watch as if you were down there yourself!

JACQUES COUSTEAU

Jacques Cousteau was a former French naval officer whose passion for the sea led him to devote the remainder of his life to exploring and protecting it. He helped to develop the Aqua-Lung, a device that allowed him to breathe underwater. He also transferred his enthusiasm to the public through a series of books, films, and television programs, becoming one of the first to popularize the undersea world. People around the world followed Cousteau's adventures, and many were inspired to begin deep-sea exploration careers of their own.

A CLOSER LOOK

One of the first and most popular missions of its kind took place from May 7 to May 22, 2014, when NOAA's *Okeanos Explorer* went on a mapping expedition along the east coast of the United States. ROVs with high-definition cameras roamed the seafloor, sending back images in real time that were free for all to view. Live-streams of this kind are only available when a mission is taking place. However, you can still watch the digitally archived versions of past missions until the next one is launched. Chances are pretty good that future deep-sea missions will offer live-streams and the opportunity to view them afterward. Just think—you could watch the next great deep-sea discovery as it happens. How incredible is that?

Okeanos Explorer's advanced video recording equipment allowed the explorers aboard to share their discoveries with audiences in real time.

SUITING UP

Atmospheric diving suits look like space suits but are waterproof and can sustain human life while the wearer is submerged. They have been around in one form or another since the early 1700s. The first diving suit was about as simple as could be. It was a wooden barrel with holes for the user's arms (sealed up with leather), a thick pane of glass for viewing, and a hose for oxygen. This simple suit was used for **salvage** operations as deep as 60 feet (18 m).

Early diving suits were very simple compared to the advanced technology used today.

A little over a century later, the next generation of diving suits started when English inventor W. H. Taylor put together the first suit with movable joints. This would allow divers greater flexibility to move their arms and legs. Taylor never actually built a usable model of his design, however. It was deemed too heavy and therefore too dangerous to wear.

GETTING BETTER ALL THE TIME

Diving-suit design improved tremendously during the 19th and 20th centuries. In 1898, a British manufacturer began producing a suit that was fairly lightweight,

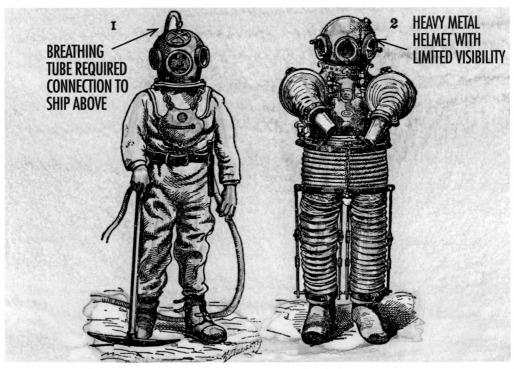

1 BREATHING TUBE REQUIRED CONNECTION TO SHIP ABOVE

2 HEAVY METAL HELMET WITH LIMITED VISIBILITY

FLEXIBLE JOINTS

CLAWS FOR
GRIPPING OBJECTS

The JIM suit reduced the amount of pressure placed on a diver's body.

allowed limb flexibility, and could withstand the pressure of relatively deep dives. Helmets were soon improved with stronger glass and multiple viewing panes. In the early 20th century, diver Benjamin Leavitt designed a suit that required no cable for oxygen. Instead, it had an oxygen tank mounted on its back.

In 1971, a British company called Underwater Marine Equipment produced the JIM suit, named in honor of veteran diver Jim Jarrett. It had fully movable joints, a communications system, and enough stability to reach incredible depths.

THE EXOSUIT

One of the most advanced suits available today is the Exosuit. The Exosuit (seen below) is designed to go deeper than any previous diving equipment. It also has rotary joints and power thrusters. This means divers can move easily and jet through the water without swimming. Perhaps most interesting of all is the suit's scuba device. It converts the carbon dioxide that a person naturally breathes out into the oxygen that's needed to breathe in. The suit features communications equipment that permits the wearer to stay in constant contact with people on the surface. This feature also allows live video feeds to be sent back in real time. ✹

CARING FOR THE PLANET

The undersea world is a vast treasure trove of resources, from a huge variety of useful plants and animals to a staggering wealth of chemicals and minerals. Of course, the appeal of learning more about these resources and how they can improve life here on the surface is tremendous. But what about the negative effects of this exploration? The marine world is vast, but its resources are limited. And in the coming years, we will become even more skilled at accessing its many treasures. As a result, one of the things we will have to decide in the future is how much of the sea's resources we should allow people to harvest. It will be important to balance the benefits of using the deep sea for our own good against the importance of preserving the planet's health.

Diamond miners use hoses to suck up dirt and rocks from the ocean floor in search of valuable stones.

FIREBOATS EQUIPPED WITH POWERFUL WATER JETS

Firefighters work to put out flames after the explosion of the Deepwater Horizon *oil rig in 2010.*

MINING OUR MANNERS

Deep-sea mining has already stirred up this controversial issue. In 2016, the first large-scale deep-sea mining operations are due to begin. These operations will provide people with huge amounts of valuable natural resources. But deep-sea mining, just like mining on land, comes at a cost. Such measures cause damage to local environments, sometimes to the point of no return.

Scientists estimate that there are anywhere from half a million to more than five million marine plant and animal species yet to be found, studied, named, and cataloged. Do we want to risk wiping out entire species and **ecosystems** before we've even had a chance to study and preserve them? This debate will undoubtedly become one of the most intense of our time as we move deeper into the last untouched frontier on our planet.

Divers explore the wreck of the USS Saratoga.

3

EARNING A PAYCHECK

F or many, fascination with the deep sea will never be anything more than a hobby. But for some people, the need to know more about what lies below the ocean waves will lead to a career in marine exploration. If you are thinking of devoting your life to studying the deepest reaches of the marine world, you will need a love of marine biology, a willingness to work hard, and a never-ending curiosity. But if you're truly dedicated, deep-sea exploration can be a rewarding career. It is also a growing field that will need many talented people in the years ahead.

PROPOSED FUTURE DEEP-SEA OBJECTIVES

2016	2016	2017	2018
The new Cyclops 3000 craft is scheduled to launch.	The first large-scale commercial deep-sea mining operations are due to begin.	Nautilus Minerals plans to open a second mining operation in the Bismarck Sea.	Earliest possible start date for oil production to begin in the Falkland Islands seabed.

LOOKING BACK

There are a lot of really old things lying around the ocean floor. Some of them were put there by nature, while others came from humans. Marine archaeologists are deep-sea explorers who make their living studying these objects. Their job begins with locating underwater archaeological sites that offer items worthy of study. A familiar example is the wreckage site of the *Titanic*, discovered in 1985 by American oceanographer Robert Ballard.

Once a site has been located, an archaeologist will plan the best way to approach it. Items that have been lying under the water for tens or even hundreds of years are very delicate. Archaeologists can't just dive down there and start pulling them up. They must therefore have expertise in how to retrieve those objects without causing them any damage. Once artifacts have been retrieved, archaeologists will lead the way in preserving and examining them. Then they will present the findings to the academic community and the public.

A diver explores a wrecked ship near the coast of Mexico.

SYLVIA EARLE

Oceanographer Sylvia Earle is a pioneer in the world of undersea exploration. In 1990, she became the first female chief scientist of NOAA, and in 1998 she was chosen as the National Geographic Society's first female explorer in residence. Earle began scuba diving while attending college during the 1950s. Since then, she has spent more than 7,000 hours underwater and led more than 100 undersea expeditions. Her work has been important in preserving the health of underwater ecosystems.

PRESERVING THE REMAINS

Once the artifacts are retrieved from the deepest parts of the ocean, some eventually find their way into museums. Others become part of academic collections. Marine archaeologists help to find and study artifacts, but who actually takes care of them once they're on the surface? A marine conservator, that's who! The conservator is the person who does most of the handling, preparation, and preservation of artifacts. This job comes with a lot of responsibility. Taking care of an item that has been resting on the seafloor for hundreds of years is no easy task.

Let's say a wooden artifact is recovered from a boat that was used by Vikings in the 900s. After sitting in the water for more than a thousand years, it has become soft. Conservators know exactly what to do to keep it from falling apart. They also decide whether it can be displayed to the public and under what conditions it should be stored under. This involves knowledge of everything from chemistry to climate control. In addition to caring for artifacts, conservators keep careful records of the items so they will be found easily when they are needed for study.

A diver examines artifacts at the wreck of the Japanese oil tanker Shinkoku Maru.

Special waterproof camera equipment enables divers to capture incredible footage.

LIGHTS, CAMERA, ACTION!

Today's video technology allows every moment of a deep-sea adventure to be presented in vivid detail. As a result, underwater filmmakers and photographers have become an important part of deep-sea exploration teams. These workers rely heavily on creative thinking. Filming underwater isn't just a matter of getting into a submersible vehicle with a camcorder. Scripts must be written, shooting strategies must be planned out, and footage must be edited. Every dive presents a unique challenge. For example, how do you best capture the image of a school of beautiful fish when your subject doesn't want to get too close to you? How do you properly light an area of the sea that has never seen light before? By coming up with creative solutions to these questions, underwater filmmakers can produce documentary material that will educate and inspire the public.

An engineer carefully draws a submersible design.

WHAT SHOULD IT LOOK LIKE?

Designing the appearance of a deep-sea submersible can be tricky. It's not a matter of simply coming up with a design that looks good. A submersible's design must serve the purpose of the vehicle. The designer has to figure out where the vehicle's equipment should go. Where will the lights be? What about the robotic arms? What's the best place for the command capsule where the pilot sits? For the controls? The computers? The designers who find the answers to these questions must walk the fine line between creativity and practicality.

ENVISIONING IT

When you think of deep-sea exploration team members, you might not think of graphic artists. However, these creative professionals often play a critical role in bringing the fascinating world beneath the waves to the wider public. Even with the power of digital cameras, it is sometimes difficult to communicate the awesome beauty of the undersea world. A graphic artist can spot a key moment when it comes—that instant when creature and environment join to form a truly mind-blowing image—and then capture it through drawings and paintings. Such artwork can spark the imagination and curiosity of people around the world. ✴

A graphic artist sketches out a design on a touch screen.

LIFE AS WE KNOW IT

Marine biology is the study of the ocean's living things. Some marine biologists choose to focus on the animals of the deep sea. These scientists are a critical part of deep-sea exploration. A deep-sea biologist studies not only the life-forms that we have known about for some time, but also those that have been recently discovered. They examine specimens and try to draw conclusions about the animals based on their appearance, general behavior, and natural environment. They also study distribution, feeding habits, life cycles, and much more.

The information they gather can be tremendously beneficial to both the human race and the organisms they study. When a new medical treatment is developed from some compound found in a deep-sea animal, for example, you can bet a marine biologist was involved. At the same time, data from the same organism can go a long way in determining how best to preserve its natural environment. Another rewarding aspect of the job is that a deep-sea biologist gets to travel and see some of the world's most amazing sights.

A marine biologist gets up close and personal with a manatee.

WATERPROOF PEN AND PAPER FOR UNDERWATER NOTE TAKING

An ecologist measures the growth of an underwater plant.

IT'S ALL ABOUT RELATIONSHIPS

Another type of scientist who plays a big role in deep-sea exploration is the marine ecologist. Ecology is the study of an organism's relationship with its environment and the other life-forms that live there. You may have heard the saying, "We're all in this together." This is certainly true of the animals that live in the deepest parts of the ocean. When something affects one of them, it almost always affects the others. A marine ecologist can learn a great deal about an undersea environment by studying how one fish reacts to another or the way a crustacean favors living in one place over someplace else. This kind of information can go a long way toward filling the gaps in our overall knowledge of the deep seas.

Marine ecologists do not spend all of their time in laboratories or on information-gathering missions, though. They may present findings to governments to help them form sensible laws for protecting marine life. Some marine ecologists might also work with companies to come up with strategies for using deep-sea resources without causing environmental damage.

Dr. Amy Baco-Taylor is an associate professor of oceanography at Florida State University.

When did you start thinking about getting into the field of deep-sea exploration? What was it about this discipline that interested/inspired you? Between my last two years of college, I got to do an NSF [National Science Foundation] Research Experience for Undergraduates program (like an internship) with a professor who did deep-sea research. I ended up doing my PhD with that same professor. I did my first sub dive for my graduate research on the day I was supposed to graduate from college. I was immediately hooked on deep-sea biology, and the science that seemed like fantasy became reality for me.

What kinds of classes did you take in high school and beyond in order to prepare for your career? In high school I was in the honors program, which meant I had to take biology, chemistry, and physics. Then my senior year, I got to take AP biology. These classes helped me get into college, but the classes that really prepared me more are the ones I took in college. I think I took almost every biology class the department offered. I also had to take a lot of chemistry, including organic chemistry and biochemistry. My work includes a lot of genetics, and I was also able to take classes in molecular biology.

What other projects and jobs did you do in school and your work life before beginning your career? And how did that work prepare you? In college I had several work-study jobs. My second year, I started working in the labs of professors in the biology department. I worked in one lab helping with literature reviews but also occasionally got to do a little bit of fieldwork and some sorting of invertebrates from mud samples. In another lab, I was sorting larval fish samples, and in the last lab I worked on proofreading an invertebrate zoology CD-ROM tutorial written by one of the professors. Through all my work-study experiences, I learned a lot about marine biology, invertebrates, and fieldwork.

Do you have a particular project that you're especially proud of or that you think really took your work to another level? That's a tough one to answer because with each project, you are trying to take your work to another level. If I have to pick one, I think probably the first proposal I got funded would be the best example. As a third-year graduate student, I was able to work on population genetics of deep-sea corals.

It was very exciting to get my first experience as a chief scientist and to get to be in charge of where the sub went for the first time! More importantly, those first deep-sea coral dives provided me with a window into the amazing communities that are found in deep-sea coral beds. The questions I thought of in those first few dives in the coral beds are still the ones that drive my research 15 years later!

It obviously takes teamwork to make things happen in the field of deep-sea exploration. Does working as part of a team come naturally to you, or was it something you had to learn and work on? Often in the media scientists are portrayed as standalone figures, but scientists would not be where they are without the contributions of all of their team members. I like to be a part of a team, and I really enjoy the team atmosphere that is created when we are out doing fieldwork.

What would your dream project be if you were given unlimited resources? I actually have a project that was recently funded for work in the far Northwestern Hawaiian Islands and into the Emperor Seamount Chain. The goal is to look at how long it takes for deep-sea corals on seamounts to recover from trawling impacts. This project combines both exploration and hypothesis-driven science, and is one that I have wanted to do for a really long time, but it has taken a really long time to get funded.

What advice would you give to a young person who wants to one day do what you do? Follow your dreams. All those cool things you see marine biologists doing in nature specials and documentaries are being done by real people right now. There's no reason you can't be one of them. ✺

A research scientist uses a microscope to study sea horses.

DATA MASTERS

Traveling down into the deepest parts of the sea is all about one thing—collecting information. But what happens after biologists and ecologists have gathered and processed their data? That's where research scientists enter the picture. Research scientists might take part in the exploration of the deep seas. More importantly, however, they work with the information after it's collected. They continue pulling out data from the evidence—everything from plant and animal specimens to sediment and water samples—and then decide what the information means.

Research scientists need to look through all the data to find what others don't. They need to spot patterns and understand what they mean. They also have to be able to figure how the information can be best applied elsewhere. For example, they think about how a chemical compound found in a certain fish could be used in the production of a new medication, or what kind of new equipment might be needed to study a certain species. So, much like a detective, a research scientist not only helps gather the evidence, but also figures out what to do with it.

CRUISING AROUND

The first step in exploring a deep-sea environment is getting there. Operating a submersible vehicle is a complex process. The scientists who study the deep seas generally aren't the ones at the controls. The people who drive these incredible vehicles are called submersible pilots. These pilots don't really do much from an academic standpoint—their job is to clear the way for the people who do. But before each dive, they have to make sure the submersible is in peak working order. They check not just the vehicle itself but also all the scientific equipment onboard. Once the dive begins, the pilot monitors the submersible's many systems, from electronics and life support to communications, cameras, and robotics. There are some desk-job aspects to the position—paperwork and other record-keeping are required before and after each dive. But most of a pilot's time is spent in the field. During a mission, a pilot may be away from home for weeks at a time. The payoff, however, is the privilege of seeing the undersea world firsthand.

Operators pilot the DeepSee craft in the Pacific Ocean.

James Cameron speaks to the crowd in front of his DEEPSEA CHALLENGER submersible.

CHAPTER FOUR

THE GREATEST CHALLENGE OF ALL . . . SO FAR

Planning and carrying out a deep-sea exploration mission is a complex process. A great deal of research and preparation must be done to ensure that the people diving underwater can safely accomplish their goals. This process can take months or even years, and it takes huge sums of money to pull off successfully. As a result, major deep-sea exploration missions don't happen every day. One of the most remarkable deep-sea achievements in recent years has been Canadian explorer and filmmaker James Cameron's 2012 journey to the deepest point on Earth. In leading the design and construction process for the *DEEPSEA CHALLENGER* submersible, Cameron not only made history but set the standard for future undersea missions.

TREMENDOUS TECHNOLOGY

1620	1715	1930	1942
The first working submarine is built.	The first practical diving helmet with an oxygen hose is invented.	The bathysphere is first used.	The first successful self-contained underwater breathing apparatus (scuba) is invented.

THE IDEA

Like all deep-sea exploration missions, Cameron's project started with an idea. Though Cameron is best known for making blockbuster Hollywood films such as *Avatar*, *Titanic*, and *The Abyss*, he has also made a name for himself in the oceanography community. Ever since he was a young boy, he was fascinated with the undersea world. His success in the movie world gave him the resources and flexibility to follow his dream of exploring the ocean depths. When it came time to plan his undersea projects, he decided that he wanted to make important contributions to deep-sea science and technology. Never

one to let an obstacle stand in his way, he decided to tackle a huge project—finding a reliable and efficient way to explore the very deepest parts of the ocean. To do that, he knew he would have to design and build a submersible craft unlike any other. The project would be expensive, time-consuming, and difficult, but it would also change deep-sea exploration forever.

James Cameron's 1989 film The Abyss *was a fictional adventure about deep-sea explorers.*

In 2001, James Cameron visited the wreck of the Titanic *to film a documentary called* Ghosts of the Abyss.

THE TEAM

As expedition leader, Cameron knew he would need help with such an ambitious project. From making big-budget films that employed thousands of people, he understood the importance of teamwork. Together with Australian engineer Ron Allum, Cameron founded a company called Acheron to build the incredible new submersible he had in mind. Allum had been working with Cameron since 2001 on various undersea projects. When Cameron explored deep-sea vents in the Atlantic and Pacific Oceans in 2004, he used systems that Allum had created. And Russian scientists used Allum's broadcast systems in their famed submersible *Mir*. It was this technology that enabled the *Mir* to send back beautiful, high-definition images of the *Titanic* wreckage from 12 separate cameras. Allum was an explorer himself, with extensive experience in cave diving—piloting submersibles into treacherous undersea cave networks. In addition to Allum, Cameron recruited a number of other engineers, divers, and scientists to join the *DEEPSEA CHALLENGER* team. With his leadership and the combined skills and experience of the team members, the project was in very good hands.

WHERE THE MAGIC HAPPENS

WOODS HOLE OCEANOGRAPHIC INSTITUTION

Of all the institutions that explore the deep seas, one of the most famous is the Woods Hole Oceanographic Institution (WHOI). Founded in 1930, it is today the largest private, nonprofit oceanographic organization in the United States. It boasts a combined staff and student body of more than 1,000 people and is located primarily in the town of Woods Hole, Massachusetts. Its stated mission is to gain a better understanding of the world's oceanic environments and use that information to improve humankind and its relationship with the marine world. WHOI uses a fleet of vessels, both on the surface and submersible, to conduct its research. It has led the design of numerous technological advancements. Some of its most notable projects include participating in the discovery of the *Titanic* in 1985 and the wreckage of Air France Flight 447 in 2011.

The submersible Alvin *returns to the WHOI ship* Atlantis II *after an undersea mission.*

A researcher studies lionfish from aboard an OceanGate submersible.

THE NATIONAL OCEANIC AND ATMOSPHERIC ADMINISTRATION

Another high-profile organization in the marine exploration community is the National Oceanic and Atmospheric Administration (NOAA). Unlike WHOI, NOAA is not a private organization. It is part of the United States government. One of NOAA's central missions is to collect and share data concerning the condition of the oceans. This information aids in everything from weather prediction to commerce and travel. NOAA also oversees the general use of U.S. coastal and oceanic environments. This means it is responsible for making sure that marine animals are not overharvested, habitats are not destroyed, and endangered species are protected. They also run programs to inform and educate the public about the importance of conserving marine communities.

OCEANGATE INC.

There are few things more exciting than being able to dive to the deepest parts of the ocean—but who exactly designs and builds the crafts that enable us to do this? One of the main companies responsible is known as OceanGate. OceanGate creates submersibles for military, governmental, academic, and private organizations. The company's services extend beyond the creation of undersea submersibles. They also include filmmaking and photography, equipment testing, data sampling and collecting, and more. The company places a particular emphasis on developing new approaches that keep up with the rapidly growing human ambition to explore the undersea world. This places it on the cutting edge of today's technology. Its new *Cyclops* series of submersibles—including the 500 and 3000 models—are currently in development and should be ready for the high seas in 2016. ✴

The interior of the DEEPSEA CHALLENGER *is very small, allowing room for only a single operator.*

THE PRESSURE

Cameron and his team knew that the biggest challenge in building the *DEEPSEA CHALLENGER* would be enabling it to withstand the unbelievable water pressure at the bottom of the Mariana Trench. Numerous other submersibles had been destroyed by such pressure without descending nearly as far as Cameron planned. There would be no room for engineering miscalculations. The pilot sphere—basically a hollow ball where the pilot sits—had to be virtually indestructible. Cameron ultimately decided to make the pilot sphere just 43 inches (1.1 m) in diameter. Along with the other equipment it would carry, this left room for just one human occupant: Cameron himself, who would pilot the submersible.

After the sphere was completed, it was tested in laboratory conditions under the stress of 16,500 pounds (7,484 kilograms) per square inch of pressure. This was equal to what the submersible would encounter at the deepest part of the ocean. It did not suffer any damage.

THE STRENGTH

Another of the key challenges in making the *DEEPSEA CHALLENGER* was to strike the perfect balance between lightness and strength. While the craft was sure to be heavy (the final model ended up weighing several tons), making it as light as possible would reduce the amount of energy it used. But what kind of material can be light, yet powerful enough to withstand the crushing pressure of the deep sea? After much trial and error, Allum created a new kind of foam to fill the empty spaces in the *DEEPSEA CHALLENGER*'s structure. It was made from tiny, hollow glass spheres and fibers. The foam had the strength needed to hold the vessel together, yet was light enough to keep the stress on its systems to a minimum. This miraculous foam was named Isofloat™. It has since been used in the construction of everything from tools to automobiles and airplanes.

Cameron presents the DEEPSEA CHALLENGER *to an audience at the California Science Center in 2013.*

This empty ballast tank is filled with water when its ship needs to descend deeper into the ocean.

CARRY THAT WEIGHT

Most aspects of deep-sea exploration technology have changed over the years, from the materials used to build ships to the sensors and other technology used to gather information. But one item has been a critical part of every undersea journey since the beginning—the ballast. Ballast is the weight that enables a submersible to sink under the surface. Without ballast, the air inside the submersible would cause the vessel to float on the surface. But once the ballast is onboard, the craft begins to gradually sink downward, enabling the journey to begin. Ballast is stored in the lower parts of a vessel, inside structures called ballast tanks, where it pulls the craft down with the aid of gravity.

WHATEVER IT TAKES

Ballast can be made up of a variety of materials. Deep-sea explorers have used many different substances throughout history. The only requirement is that the ballast has enough weight to pull the craft down. Everything from stones, sand, and soil to iron, lead, and even water have been used as ballast. The amount of ballast must be weighed very carefully to make sure the submersible descends at a reasonable rate. Sometimes a vessel only needs to submerge to a certain depth and then remain there, suspended. And with pressure increasing rapidly during descent, the craft should not be allowed to drop down too quickly. Even a very strong vessel needs time to gradually adapt to pressure changes. Also, if there is more than one ballast hold, each needs to be filled relatively equally. Otherwise, there is a risk that the craft will descend in a lopsided fashion.

WHAT GOES DOWN MUST GO UP

After a submersible has reached its destination and all research has been performed, the amount of ballast is adjusted so the craft can begin its ascent. Again, this has to be done gradually, as there are many dangers to climbing too fast. Ballast can be removed from its tanks by simple release, where a panel opens and allows it to tumble out into the water. Other times, it is forced out and replaced with air. Environmental groups have taken a stand against some forms of ballast, pointing out that certain materials can cause environmental damage when dumped. As a result of these concerns, many submersibles now use rocks and sand that are native to their research area, or simply fill their ballast holds with seawater. Thus, the age of using junk material as ballast is likely at an end. ✳

Ballast water is often emptied through special valves on the side of a vessel.

THE OTHER STUFF

The *DEEPSEA CHALLENGER* was also equipped with countless other features that put it on the edge of modern technology. The submersible was propelled by 12 separate thrusters, both horizontal and vertical. This allowed the vessel to easily move in any direction at speeds of roughly 3.5 miles (5.6 km) per hour. This may not sound like much, but it was, in fact, quite fast for a craft of this type. The batteries powered not just the propulsion system but everything else as well. In spite of significant demands, the ship's batteries could power its systems for more than 50 hours.

Interestingly, in spite of its elongated shape, the *DEEPSEA CHALLENGER* was designed to move about vertically rather than using more traditional horizontal, submarine-like movements. This would allow the craft to descend more rapidly to maximize time at the ocean's bottom for exploration. The submersible's descent speed was also enhanced by its enormous amount of ballast—more than 1,000 pounds (453.6 kg).

A model of the DEEPSEA CHALLENGER is displayed alongside a photo of Cameron at an event in Italy.

The DEEPSEA CHALLENGER *undergoes testing in waters off the shores of Australia.*

THE TESTS

Once the *DEEPSEA CHALLENGER* was assembled, Cameron and his team decided it was time to "go operational" and dive the sub in open water. These dives took place between January and March 2012 and afforded the team an opportunity to identify and address engineering problems while conducting scientific research in rarely or never-before-explored places, such as the New Britain Trench off the coast of Papua New Guinea. For each dive, the team took the craft progressively deeper—first down to about 3,200 feet (975 m), then to just under 24,000 feet (7,315 m), and finally to 27,000 feet (8,230 m). They encountered numerous problems along the way. In mid-February, for example, there were issues with both the camera systems and the life-support systems. During another test, the power systems began working incorrectly. A third test revealed flaws in the vertical thrusters, forcing Cameron to return to the surface earlier than planned. The team was no doubt frustrated by these difficulties. However, they also knew that such issues were to be expected when working with new technology in such challenging environments.

Cameron has a final discussion with his team before closing the hatch and beginning his dive.

THE DIVE

Once the major technical issues had been resolved, it was time to make history and become the first solo pilot to dive to the deepest place on Earth. By mid-March, Cameron felt that the sub he'd co-created was ready to fulfill its primary mission of exploring and studying the Mariana Trench. The ship carrying the craft reached its position over the deepest part of the Mariana Trench during the night of March 25. With Cameron at the controls, the craft was set into the water, and it finally began its descent. Cameron stayed in constant communication with the team on the surface. The *DEEPSEA CHALLENGER*'s systems also sent critical data back to the ship automatically every three minutes, in case something happened to Cameron or the craft's communications systems.

THE VICTORY

It took Cameron and the *DEEPSEA CHALLENGER* exactly two hours and 37 minutes to reach the seafloor—less than half the time it took *Trieste* in 1960. Cameron remained at the bottom for about three hours, as opposed to *Trieste*'s 20 minutes. Not everything worked as planned. For example, in the face of the unsurpassed water pressure at Challenger Deep, some of the machines for collecting samples refused to function. But for the most part, the *DEEPSEA CHALLENGER* performed magnificently, enabling Cameron to reach a maximum depth of 35,787 feet (10,908 m) and capture some astonishing images of unprecedented quality. Many of these images were used in the production of a breathtaking documentary of the trip called *DEEPSEA CHALLENGE 3D*. In addition, the submersible collected water, small life-forms, and other samples to be analyzed later by scientists.

On March 26, 2013, the first anniversary of his dive to the Challenger Deep, Cameron donated the *DEEPSEA CHALLENGER* submersible and science platform to WHOI to facilitate further improvements to its platform and their incorporation into other deep-sea submersibles. Through hard work and careful planning, he and his team have conquered one of deep-sea exploration's biggest challenges.

WHOI will use the DEEPSEA CHALLENGER *to continue exploring previously unseen parts of the ocean.*

People have dumped large amounts of trash into the world's oceans, causing huge damage to the water and the life-forms that live there.

BENEFITS BIG AND SMALL

Countless organizations, from government agencies to nonprofit firms to corporations, have their own plans for the bottom of the ocean. Some are in search of chemicals and minerals that can be used to produce everything from cosmetics and medicine to energy. Others have plans to develop underwater tourism programs. Even as you read this, there are teams of engineers designing equipment with the purpose of establishing a human presence in the deepest reaches of the waters. There is little doubt that the seabed—some of the planet's last undiscovered territory—represents a vast kingdom of untapped wealth.

STRIKING A BALANCE

As with any other resource, humans have a responsibility to try to strike the perfect balance between using the deep sea for their own benefit and ruining its natural state. Many experts are already gravely concerned about this. They are trying to provide a sensible voice in the discussion before the problem gets out of hand. These people are helping to explain the importance of reducing oceanic trash-dumping and lowering the amount of air pollution caused by ocean exploitation. Others are calling for an end

Without regulations, commercial fishing can damage the environment by harvesting too many fish.

to **poaching** and unregulated commercial fishing, restrictions on offshore oil and gas exploration, and a ban on other activities that could damage the environment. Whether any or all of these things come to pass, it is clear that regulations will be needed to protect the ocean depths from overuse.

THE ROAD AHEAD

James Cameron's historic dive in March 2012 helped renew many people's interest in the possibilities of deep-sea exploration. The findings from Cameron's mission have already been presented at numerous academic conferences, and the *DEEPSEA CHALLENGER* has set a new standard for future submersibles. In the few years that have passed since the mission, microbiologists have discovered dozens of new species collected during the dive, with literally thousands more samples yet to be examined. Some experts even believe that evidence collected during the mission could alter our existing theories on the evolution of life, not only on Earth but also on other planets. Considering the further promise of advancements in everything from medical treatment to the manufacture of building materials, there is no doubt that deep-sea exploration will continue to be a key activity in the 21st century. ✴

Offshore oil and gas rigs cause pollution and environmental damage.

CAREER STATS

GEOSCIENTISTS

MEDIAN ANNUAL SALARY (2012): $90,890

NUMBER OF JOBS (2012): 38,200

PROJECTED JOB GROWTH: 16%, faster than average

PROJECTED INCREASE IN JOBS 2012–2022: 6,000

REQUIRED EDUCATION: Bachelor's degree needed for most entry-level positions; PhD is required for many jobs

LICENSE/CERTIFICATION: May be required for certain jobs

MARINE ENGINEERS AND NAVAL ARCHITECTS

MEDIAN ANNUAL SALARY (2012): $88,100

NUMBER OF JOBS (2012): 7,300

PROJECTED JOB GROWTH: 10%, average

PROJECTED INCREASE IN JOBS 2012–2022: 800

REQUIRED EDUCATION: Bachelor's degree

LICENSE/CERTIFICATION: May be required for certain jobs

ZOOLOGISTS AND WILDLIFE BIOLOGISTS

MEDIAN ANNUAL SALARY (2012): $57,710

NUMBER OF JOBS (2012): 20,100

PROJECTED JOB GROWTH: 5%, slower than average

PROJECTED INCREASE IN JOBS 2012–2022: 1,000

REQUIRED EDUCATION: Bachelor's degree needed for most entry-level positions; PhD is required for many jobs

LICENSE/CERTIFICATION: May be required for certain jobs

Figures reported by the United States Bureau of Labor Statistics

RESOURCES

BOOKS

Johnson, Jinny. *Deep Sea Life*. Mankato, MN: Smart Apple Media, 2012.

Johnson, Rebecca L. *Journey into the Deep: Discovering New Ocean Creatures*. Minneapolis: Millbrook Press, 2011.

Rodríguez, Ana María. *Leatherback Turtles, Giant Squids, and Other Mysterious Animals of the Deepest Seas*. Berkeley Heights, NJ: Enslow, 2012.

Spilsbury, Richard. *Deep Sea Exploration*. New York: Crabtree Publishing Co., 2011.

FACTS FOR NOW

Visit this Scholastic Web site for more information on deep-sea exploration:
www.factsfornow.scholastic.com
Enter the keywords **Deep-Sea Exploration**

GLOSSARY

bathysphere (BATH-iss-feer) a spherical craft designed to sustain a human crew at great underwater depths

buoyant (BOY-uhnt) able to float or stay afloat

ecosystems (EE-koh-sis-tuhmz) all the living things in a place and their environment

fathom (FATH-uhm) a unit for measuring how deep the water is; 1 fathom equals 6 feet (1.8 m)

implode (im-PLOHD) burst inward

maneuverable (muh-NOO-vur-uh-buhl) able to make precise, accurate movements

nautical (NAW-ti-kuhl) of or having to do with ships or sailing

oceanography (oh-shuh-NAH-gruh-fee) the scientific study of the ocean and the plants and animals that live in it

poaching (POH-ching) hunting or fishing illegally on someone else's property

pressure (PRESH-ur) the force produced by pressing on something, as in water pressure

salvage (SAL-vij) property rescued from a shipwreck, fire, flood, or other disaster

sonar (SOH-nahr) an instrument used on ships and submarines that sends out underwater sound waves to determine the location of objects and the distance to the bottom

specimens (SPES-uh-muhnz) samples of or from living things, or examples used to stand in for a whole group, as in a butterfly specimen or a blood specimen

submersible (suhb-MUR-suh-bul) a vessel designed to travel underwater for reasonably long periods of exploration

INDEX

Page numbers in *italics* indicates illustrations.

INDEX *(CONTINUED)*

ABOUT THE AUTHOR

WIL MARA'S fascination with marine exploration began as a child growing up along the shores of New Jersey and watching the famed Jacques Cousteau on his hit TV series *The Undersea World of Jacques Cousteau*, which ran in the 1960s and 1970s. Wil is the award-winning, best-selling author of more than 150 books, many of which are educational titles for children.